Primary Source

PRIMARY
SOURCE

poems

Jason Schneiderman

RED HEN PRESS | PASADENA, CA

Book layout by Latina Vidolova

Library of Congress Cataloging-in-Publication Data

Names: Schneiderman, Jason, author.
Title: Primary source / Jason Schneiderman.
Description: First edition. | Pasadena, CA : Red Hen Press, [2016]
Identifiers: LCCN 2015046624 | ISBN 9781597097437 (softcover)
Subjects: | BISAC: POETRY / General.
Classification: LCC PS3619.C4473 A6 2016 | DDC 811/.6—dc23
LC record available at http://lccn.loc.gov/2015046624

The National Endowment for the Arts, the Los Angeles County Arts Commission, the
Los Angeles Department of Cultural Affairs, the Dwight Stuart Youth Fund, the Pasa-
dena Arts & Culture Commission and the City of Pasadena Cultural Affairs Division, Sony
Pictures Entertainment, and Ahmanson Foundation partially support Red Hen Press.

First Edition
Published by Red Hen Press
www.redhen.org

Acknowledgments

I am grateful to the editors of the journals and magazines where the following poems first appeared:

American Academy of Poets Poem-A-Day: "Sita," "Vocabulary;" *American Poetry Review*: "If You Died," "The Sadness of Antonio," "White Boy;" *Court Green*: "Alternate Side of the Street Parking," "Anachronistic Fair Use Self Portraits of 20th Century Sylvia Plath (with 'Daddy' fixation)," "My Rich Friend," "On First Looking into Ashbery's Self-Portrait," "On Last Looking into Ashbery's Self-Portrait," "To Please and Instruct," "Pornography III," "Schuyler-esque," "Self Portrait of Gertrude Stein with Increasing Plath Fixation;" *Ducts*: "In the Style of the Master," "Overheard in the Diner;" *Forklift, Ohio*: "The Worst Children's Book Ever;" *Lambda Literary Review*: "The Turing Test;" *McSweeney's*: "The Buffy Sestina;" *Mipoesias*: "Self Portrait of the Artist as a Young Sex Object (Age 19);" *Prairie Schooner*: "Tyra Hunter;" *Spork*: "10 Poems for Fluxus;" *Story Quarterly*: "Pornography II: The Capacity to Love."

For Jen and Ada

Contents

III

Primary Source

I

You're the top!
You're a high that's mellow
You're the top!
You're a P-Town Fellow
You're the changing light
of James Merrill's sprite
who told him of his soul!
You're Helen Vendler
You're Stephen Spender
You're Yoko Ono's fol-de-rol!
You're the top!
You're Shakespeare's heather
You're the top!
You're Thom Gunn's leather
I'm a tone deaf singer, a dying zinger, a David Lee Roth be-bop!
But if baby I'm the bottom, you're the top!

THE SADNESS OF ANTONIO

In sooth, I know not why I am so sad
—The opening line of *The Merchant of Venice*, spoken by Antonio

We approach The Merchant of Venice *with a question (Why is Antonio sad?)* . . .
—James Longenbach, *The Resistance to Poetry*

I will argue here that The Merchant *deliberately frustrates any possibility of identification with its characters...*
—James O'Rourke,
"Racism and Homophobia in *The Merchant of Venice*"

Antonio, we should remind ourselves,
        is not real.

He is not in the body of the actor
        or the words on the page,

and yet we return to the question:
        Why is he sad?

There is no Antonio in the way
        for instance

there is a homeless man
        outside the subway,

his clothes made out of
        newspapers, folded

to ribbons and tied into bows.
        We would not

call him sad.
          We would call him crazy.

We avoid his eyes,
          we avoid his stench,

but he is there.
          He is there.

There is no Antonio
          in the way

that there are ten fifth graders
          placed under my tutelage

and brought to a production of
          The Merchant of Venice

because the fifth grade drama class
          always sees

whatever the Manhattan Summer Shakespeare Group
          is putting on.

The next morning,
          writing earnestly in their journals,

they find themselves
          entirely offended.

As a Jew,
        one writes,

I was deeply offended
        by the behavior

in the play
        toward Shylock.

The quality of self-righteousness
        is not strained.

I think it was wrong,
        writes a stocky blond boy,

to be mean to someone
        for his race.

Then he crosses out *race*
        and writes in

religion. Oh, children.
        This is an easy one.

Not one of them notice
        that Antonio is sad.

Antonio is entirely ignored
        in their journals.

He holds no interest
    for them.

Fine. We can do this.
    I ask what

Shylock is ridiculed
    for calling out

when Jessica elopes,
    stealing her father's money.

They don't remember,
    so I direct them in their scripts.

They find it:
    my ducats and my daughter.

I ask them what it is that Lorenzo has taken
    and as the light dawns

one girl answers,
    his ducats and his daughter!

I say,
    so the Christians want

what they ridicule Shylock
    for wanting

and slowly,
        they all see the light.

Fifth graders of the world
        unite!

This is their first experience
        of what we used to call

reading against the grain.
        They have never

read against the grain.
        They have never

felt so smart. They have never
        realized that a text

can contain its own critique.
        Fifth graders of the world,

do not spend your summer
        at school camp!

The most childlike of my children
        is built like a porcelain doll

and cries at the drop of a hat.
        He cries because the other children

are mean to him, and the other children
    are mean to him because

he treats them with disdain
    and is always about to cry.

As I comfort him
    for the third time that day

I realize how much less real
    he is to me than Antonio.

At the end of six weeks
    I will deliver this boy

back to the incompetent arms
    of his awkward parents

and rarely will he cross my mind.
    The girl who is being possessed

by puberty, whose legs are ready
    for shaving and whose armpits

are ready for deodorant,
    who hides her face in a stack

of novels that are thinly veiled
    rape fantasies for the barely

pubescent, she too is less real to me
than Antonio.

She will grow out of this.
I won't see it,

but she will learn to shave,
to groom better,

and I will rarely think about her
because she will become

a person
I will never know.

I try to ask about Antonio,
but their interest

is only in Shylock. When I was
in fifth grade,

we also read
The Merchant of Venice.

I was the only Jew in class,
and the only student,

who, given the choice,
memorized "The Quality of Mercy"

rather than "I am a Jew."
        I read the introduction

to our Bedford or Dover or
        Oxford edition

and learned about how Shakespeare
        gave Shylock a humanity

that no other Jew in Renaissance
        Drama even comes close to,

even if that humanity is not entirely
        complete. I learned a passage

that was twice as long,
        and secretly,

I learned the "I am a Jew" speech
        to see what it would feel like

to say. When we read
        the play out loud,

I read Antonio, so I felt it more
        than the others,

his sadness. Under everything
        you can feel how

he would do anything
        for Bassanio,

and yet, he knew not why he
        was sad.

These children love
        Shylock. They can't see

his racism or his cruelty,
        or rather they think

that powerlessness is panacea.
        Because they are powerless

they believe
        that to be unable

to hurt another person
        is the same as being good.

My assistant tries once more
        to interest

our children in Antonio,
        to start the conversation

that might lead to Elizabethan
        perceptions of sodomitical

subcultures as they existed
       in early modern Venice,

but without luck.
       We wonder if our students

notice how queer we are,
       and that night,

we joke about creating a 1990's version
       of *The Merchant of Venice*

that could open with Antonio
       breaking the silence

and conclude with an ACTUP!
       demonstration

in which a gender-queer Portia would insist
       on her right to body modification surgeries,

and a Derridean Jessica
       would deconstruct

the Jewish/Christian binary,
       in addition to dredging up

recovered memories
       of satanic abuse,

at the hands of Shylock.
        We make ourselves laugh,

smug in our knowledge,
        but sad in its failure,

though even that
        doesn't quite

resolve the question of why
        Antonio is sad.

Do you remember the homeless man?

He doesn't ask me for money,
        nor does he ask anyone.

He sits on the grate, and talks to himself.
        His elaborate costume

is ineluctably real. He is
        real, but he is not

my object of study. He resides
        in himself, and he cannot

be read with or against the grain.
        I do not talk to him.

He occupies my mind
        for as little time

as he is in front of me.
        Poor Antonio.

As I return to my home
        by train,

Antonio occupies my mind.
        He is nowhere at all:

Not in the past,
        not in the body

of the actor,
        not in the history

of Venice
        or England

or America.
        And still

the question returns:
        Why is Antonio sad?

I look around,
        and there is no one

to ask.

My Rich Friend

My rich friend wasn't always rich
but now he's very good at it,
by which I mean he's generous,
has excellent taste, never makes
anyone uncomfortable, has good
boundaries, and please don't tell him
but if I were ever to kill myself,
he has this wonderful window
in this perfect little dining nook
that's fifteen stories up and opens
all the way. The last thing
I would see is a soapstone zodiac
carved into a recess in the ceiling,
and then the city going by
ever so fast. I'm not usually tempted
by an open window. I don't know
how he survives it every day.

ALTERNATE SIDE OF THE STREET PARKING

I said, *I can't stop worrying about the car,*
and you said, *Because you're afraid of it*

getting hit? Or because you know you have
to move it again tomorrow? and I said, *Both,*

it's the all of it, the never being done with it,
the never having more than two days of rest

before it has to be moved again, and
it's hard to find a space, and I'm not very

good at parallel parking, and you said,
That's what being a grown up is like,

and I said, *Being afraid all the time? Never*
being finished with worry? and you said

Yes, for you, that's what being a grown up
is like for you, and I said, *But that's what*

being a child was like, being afraid, all
the time, and you said, *Well, then nothing*

has changed, and I said, *Well at least I have*
a car. Something, I said, *has to be different.*

White Boy

I was called a nigger in the Bronx.
A man walked up to me and asked
me to buy a newspaper. I ignored
him. Which felt terrible. I've read *Invisible*
Man. I knew I was denying his
humanity. But I didn't want to buy
a newspaper. I didn't want to give
him a dollar. I didn't want him to walk
alongside me until my acknowledgement
of his humanity led to an exchange
of cash. I do this all the time. I ignore
people all the time. He was walking
next to me. I was going to a school
where I was teaching children with
anger management problems. I was
trying not to listen to his pitch, trying
not to engage, and at the top of the hill
he slammed the newspaper into my
chest and said, "Take it nigger,"
which I actually found very funny.
I listen to Lil' Kim. I know he was
just using it as a synonym for "person"
or perhaps a synonym for "man."
I know he wasn't calling me into
blackness, or calling me out of humanity.
I wanted to ask, "You know what
that means where I come from, right?"
But of course he knows. I just wanted
to ask.

SELF PORTRAIT OF THE ARTIST
AS A YOUNG SEX OBJECT (AGE 19)

It was a nice body, slender,
not as flexible as you might
have hoped, fun for a few hours,
but nothing you would want
to keep or hold onto. The bodies
of young men are like
furniture from Ikea,
clean lines, smooth surfaces,
but no real promise
of longevity or staying power
and mine was no different,
and I knew that, which was
why I wanted the bodies
of older men, their skin
mapping out the place
I would go, their touch
the promise of living
into that country of age that
seemed so far away that
I thought I might never get there.
One man would tell me
nothing, except to confirm
that he was older than
my father, and this was
on the subway, the morning
after we had lain down
on his bed under a painting
of him that had been done
when he was still a model,
decades ago. He liked

my body because it reminded
him of the one he had lost.
It comforted him too,
because his had been
so much prettier.

If You Died

I'd tattoo your name
on my forearm,

in fourteen point font,
Times New Roman,

starting at the crook
of my elbow

and taking up
exactly two inches

(I've measured).

It's a stupid thing to think:
What would I do if you died?

You can't prepare
for death.

But I can love the sight
of my empty arm.

II

You're the top!
You're No Tell Motel.
You're the top!
You're Marie Howe's hair gel.
You're the odd syntax of Ashberian hacks
who want to be published in Fence.
You're Fawcett, Farah,
you're Frank O'Hara,
you're future tense!
You're the Beats,
you're a Dale Young suture.
You're the tweets,
of Ashton Kutcher.
I'm an unread novel, a Bed-Stuy hovel, a flop
but if baby, I'm the bottom, you're the top!

Vocabulary

I used to love words,
but not looking them up.

Now I love both,
the knowing,

and the looking up,
the absurdity

of discovering that "boreal"
has been meaning

"northern" all this time
or that "estrus"

is a much better word
for the times when

I would most likely
have said, "in heat."

When I was translating,
the dictionary

was my enemy,
the repository of knowledge

that I seemed incapable
of retaining. The foreign word

for "inflatable" simply
would not stay in my head,

though the English word "deictic,"
after just one encounter,

has stuck with me for a year.
I once lost "desiccated"

for a decade, first encountered
in an unkind portrayal

of Ronald Reagan, and then
finally returned to me

in an article about cheese.
I fell in love with my husband,

not when he told me
what the word "aperçu" means,

but when I looked it up,
and he was right.

There's even a word
for when you use a word

not to mean its meaning,
but as a word itself,

and I'd tell you what it was
if I could remember it.

My friend reads the dictionary
for its perspective on culture,

laughs when I say that
reference books are not really

books, but proleptic databases.
My third grade teacher

used to joke that if we were bored
we could copy pages out of the dictionary,

but when I did, also as a joke,
she was horrified rather than amused.

Discovery is always tinged
with sorrow, the knowledge

that you have been living
without something,

so we try to make learning
the province of the young,

who have less time to regret
having lived in ignorance.

My students are lost
in dictionaries,

unable to figure out why
"categorize" means

"to put into categories"
or why the fifth definition

of "standard" is the one
that will make the sentence

in question make sense.
I wonder how anyone

can live without knowing
the word "wonder."

A famous author
once said in an interview

that he ended his novel
with an obscure word

he was sure his reader
would not know

because he liked the idea
of the reader looking it up.

He wanted the reader,
upon closing his book, to open

another, that second book
being a dictionary,

and however much I may have loved
that author, after reading

that story
(and this may surprise you)

I loved him less.

Anachronistic Fair Use Self Portraits of 20th Century Sylvia Plath (with "Daddy" Fixation)

1. Self Portrait of Sylvia Plath as Raymond Roussel

Voodoo pot glue, Voodoo pot glue
Fennel ore, slack screw,
Sandwich spy salve sieved spike afoot
Forth shirty spears, boor and slight,
Warily scaring to free Pikachu.

2. Self Portrait of Sylvia Plath as Raymond Queneau (N+7, verbs, nouns, adjectives)

You dob not dob, you dob not dob
Any more, bladish shokku
In which I have lixiviated like a foozle
For thistly yellow-fish, popcorn and whizgig
Barely Darking to Breech or Achromatize.

3. Self Portrait of Sylvia Plath as F. T. Marinetti

YOU do
not
do

YOU do
not
do

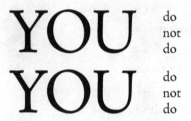

Any more black shoe

In which I have lived
like   a   foot
for   thirty   years
poor   and   white

BARELY ᴅᴀʀɪɴɢ ᴛᴏ BREATHE ᴏʀ ACHOO

4. Self Portrait of Sylvia Plath as Ludwig Wittgenstein

1. There is a Daddy
1.1 The Daddy is the case
1.2 The Daddy does not do
1.3 The Daddy does not do
1.4 The Daddy does not do anymore
1.5 The Daddy is like a shoe
2. There is a daughter
2.1 She lives in the shoe-like father
2.1.2 The daughter is foot-like
2.2 The daughter is poor
2.3 The daughter is white
2.4 The daughter has foot-like lived in the father shoe-like for thirty years
2.5 She barely dares to breath
2.6 She barely dares to achoo

5. *Self Portrait of Sylvia Plath as Tristan Tzara*

Daddy   Daddy   Daddy   Daddy   Daddy   Daddy   Daddy   Daddy
Daddy   Daddy   Daddy   Daddy   Daddy   Daddy   Daddy   Daddy
Daddy   Daddy   Daddy   Daddy   Daddy   Daddy   Daddy   Daddy
Daddy   Daddy   Daddy   Daddy   Daddy   Daddy   Daddy   Daddy
Daddy   Daddy   Daddy   Daddy   Daddy   Daddy   Daddy   Daddy
Daddy   Daddy   Daddy   Daddy   Daddy   Daddy   Daddy   Daddy
Daddy   Daddy   Daddy   Daddy   Daddy   Daddy   Daddy   Daddy
Daddy   Daddy   Daddy   Daddy   Daddy   Daddy   Daddy   Daddy
Daddy   Daddy   Daddy   Daddy   Daddy   Daddy   Daddy   Daddy
Daddy   Daddy   Daddy   Daddy   Daddy   Daddy   Daddy   Daddy
Daddy   Daddy   Daddy   Daddy   Daddy   Daddy   Daddy   Daddy
Daddy   Daddy   Daddy   Daddy   Daddy   Daddy   Daddy   Daddy
Daddy   Daddy   Daddy   Daddy   Daddy   Daddy   Daddy   Daddy
Daddy   Daddy   Daddy   Daddy   Daddy   Daddy   Daddy   Daddy
Daddy   Daddy   Daddy   Daddy   Daddy   Daddy   Daddy   Daddy
Daddy   Daddy   Daddy   Daddy   Daddy   Daddy   Daddy   Daddy
Daddy   Daddy   Daddy   Daddy   Daddy   Daddy   Daddy   Daddy
Daddy   Daddy   Daddy   Daddy   Daddy   Daddy   Daddy   Daddy
Daddy   Daddy   Daddy   Daddy   Daddy   Daddy   Daddy   Daddy
Daddy   Daddy   Daddy   Daddy   Daddy   Daddy   Daddy   Daddy
Daddy   Daddy   Daddy   Daddy   Daddy   Daddy   Daddy   Daddy
Daddy   Daddy   Daddy   Daddy   Daddy   Daddy   Daddy   Daddy
Daddy   Daddy   Daddy   Daddy   Daddy   Daddy   Daddy   Daddy
Daddy   Daddy   Daddy   Daddy   Daddy   Daddy   Daddy   Daddy
Daddy   Daddy   Daddy   Daddy   Daddy   Daddy   Daddy   Daddy
Who still considers herself very likable Sylvia Plath

To Please and Instruct

The purpose of art is to please and instruct
—Horace, *Ars Poetica*

The moral of this poem is fuck you.

The moral of this poem is I'm drunk.

The moral of this poem is I'm too drunk to be held responsible for what I'm saying to you right now.

The moral of this poem is you're fat.

The moral of this poem is if you come after me, I will have your Hotmail account turned off, true story.

The moral of this poem is herpes.

The moral of this poem is the Pope's a liar.

The moral of this poem is I'm sorry I threw up through my nose on you.

The moral of this poem is getting through customs without a passport.

The moral of this poem is gestalt therapy.

The moral of this poem is terrorists.

The moral of this poem is you like Tarantino movies because you're stupid and I like Tarantino moves because I'm smart.

The moral of this poem is cats that look like Hitler.

The moral of this poem is reality television.

The moral of this poem is don't have sex with your siblings, parents, or anyone under eighteen, sixteen if you're in Greece, fourteen in Denmark.

The moral of this poem is meth mouth.

The moral of this poem is gun-show loophole.

The moral of this poem is *Gawker*.

The moral of this poem is two state solution.

The moral of this poem is too much rage.

The moral of this poem is rehab sucks.

The moral of this poem is your wife being fingered in the bathroom at a party by this guy you invited because you thought he was cool and look where that got you.

The moral of this poem is rules change.

The moral of this poem is George Washington filling his dentures with teeth pulled from his slaves.

The moral of this poem is kill me.

The moral of this poem is hip surgery.

The moral of this poem is drone strike wedding massacre.

The moral of this poem is thong.

The moral of this poem is shut up.

The moral of this poem is make me.

Ten Poems for Fluxus (For Private Reading or Public Performance)

I. Poem for John Cage (I)

II. Restoring the Contract Modernism Broke

(Ask everyone in the audience to stand up and turn to their right. Ask them to turn to the back. Ask them to continue in their revolution until they are facing forward again, and then to take their seats. If you are alone, undertake these actions yourself.)

III. Erasing the Line between Art & Life

(On this page write down three things you have eaten today. Do this every time you come to this page, even if you have already written the three things today, or someone else has. Insert a line break after every item of food. If you are reading this to a group, ask them to call out the things they have eaten today, and write down the first three items you can understand.)

IV. Meditating on the Line Between Art & Life

(On this page, write whether you think that the poem you wrote in section III should be considered a poem—briefly elaborate. For performance, take a simple yes/no vote and record the numbers and the date of the vote on this page.)

V. Poem for John Cage (II)

(Slowly count to ten on your fingers. If you have fewer or more than ten fingers, count to however many fingers you have. If you are reading to an audience, do not explain what you are doing.)

VI. Reviving Poetry with the Thrill of the Naughty

(Take off one article of clothing. Ask your audience to do the same.)

VII. Expanding the Genre-Limited Boundaries of Poems

(Draw a circle on the page. Now a triangle. Now a rectangle. Do not let their lines touch or cross over each other. Do this each time you come to this page. If you are reading to an audience, tell them what you are you doing, but do not show them.)

VIII. Remembering the Material Nature of the Body

(Spit on this page. Let it dry. If you are too delicate to spit, you may lick the page. But it is very important to let the page dry before turning. In performance, ask a volunteer to lick the page. You may want to have a second copy of this book handy so that you can continue reading while still letting the page dry.)

IX. Isolating the Subject from Any Idea of the Real

(Close your eyes, and press on your closed eyelids. The colors you see are the poem. Ask the audience to do the same.)

X. Hyperoxygenation

(Tear off a piece of this page. Burn it.)

SELF PORTRAIT OF GERTRUDE STEIN WITH INCREASING PLATH FIXATION

For David & Byron (Every Night!)

1. (from "Custard")

a.

Sylvia is this. It has Sylvias, Sylvias, when. Not to be. Not to be narrowly. This makes a while little Sylvia.

b.

Sylvia Sylvias this. It Sylvias Sylvias, Sylvias, when. Not to Sylvia. Not to Sylvia narrowly. This Sylvias a while little Sylvia.

c.

Sylvia Sylvias Sylvia. Sylvia Sylvias, Sylvias, Sylvias, Sylvia. Sylvia to Sylvia. Sylvia to Sylviva, Slyvialy. Sylvia Sylvia a Sylvia Sylvia Sylvia.

2. *(from "A purse")*

a.

A Plath was not green, it was not straw color, it was hardly Plath, and it has a use a long Plath and the Plath, the Plath was never missing, it was not misplaced, it showed that it was open, that is all that it showed.

b.

A Plath was not Plath, it was not Plath color, it was hardly Plath, and it has a use a Plath Plath and the Plath, the Plath was never Plathing, it was not misPlathed, it Plathed that it was Plath, that is all that it Plathed.

c.

A Plath Plath not Plath, Plath Plath not Plath color, Plath was Plathly Plath, and Plath Plath a Plath a Plath Plath and the Plath, the Plath Plath never Plathing, Plath Plath not misPlathed, Plath Plathed that Plath Plath Plath, Plath Plath all that Plath Plathed.

Safe(r) Prosody /
Erotic Errata

For "syntax,"
say "latex."

For "speaker"
say "squeaker."

Alliteration is
annihilation

when
you say

"bare-backing bards
are beguiling the bug"

or

"gift giving gays
are gagging on…

gags?"

You miss the silence,
now it's broken.

You miss the ride,
the subway token.

Try:

"That's no metaphor,
that's my infection."

Try:

"That's no illness,
that's my erection."

Instead of "anxiety"
say "satiety."

Instead of "influence"
say "flu-like symptoms."

It's only fun
when you do it too;

when we do it
alone with cameras,

and then share.

Theology

Q: To fear God is to _____ Satan.

    A. fear
    B. love
    C. hate
    D. detest

Answer Key:

If you chose A, you may be a recent convert, and recently escaped from Satan's very clutches, which can be a harrowing experience; though really, despite what you may have seen in movies like *The Exorcist*, Satan's power is really quite limited, and you need not experience fear.

If you chose B, you are taking God's advice very literally and loving your enemy, for which we commend you. We do wonder, though, if you are simply giving us the answer we want to hear, or whether there is indeed truly love in your heart for the father of all lies.

We do have to object to answer C. Hate is actually the beginning of love for Satan. You do not defeat the darkness by letting it into your heart.

Answer D is fairly close, but still not correct.

The correct answer was not included, and that is the test. If you need us to tell you how to feel toward Satan, then you are lost. When you are tempted, we will not be present. We hope you are not lost. Still: It's never too late to be found.

III

You're the top!
You're Pinsky thinking.
You're the top!
You're Bishop drinking.
You're the red hot sex
that Mark Doty gets
in essays, memoirs and poems!
You're Logan's takedowns,
you're Lowell's breakdowns,
you're garden gnomes!
You're the top,
you're the wife of Ted Hughes.
You're the top,
you're William Matthews.
I'm the endless ramble of an unplanned panel at A.W.P. or "awp"!
But if baby I'm the bottom, you're the top.

Pornography II:
The Capacity to Love

These naked girls really love animals
in ways that I just don't. My therapist
thinks it's because I never had pets
growing up. These naked girls must have
had pets, but not clothes. That's how
they grew with the capacity for animal love
in the buff. I only grew up with the capacity
for didacticism and fear, bitterness,
the ability to judge myself by what I can't do.

Like what that girl is doing with a donkey—
I couldn't do that. I'm not flexible enough
or dedicated enough. My therapist wants me
to work things out with my Dad, but really,
I think I need the unconditional love of a dog
or monkey. I think that's what would set me
on the right path. Did these girls have weird
displaced Oedipal complexes that they somehow
brought to their afterschool job at the stable?

I'm sorry, women have Electra complexes.
I'm the one who couldn't get it Oedipal.
If I had managed an Oedipal complex,
I would get to be straight, but gay as I am,
I'm not gay enough to take a donkey cock

like that. My therapist says I'm a narcissist,
and I guess it's true, because that girl's
fucking a donkey and all I can talk about
is myself.

The Turing Test

It might be urged that when playing 'the imitation game' the best strategy for the machine may possibly be something other than the behaviour of a man.
—Alan Turing

Who do you think he is, this boy in the Midwest
jerking off to the end of Alan Turing's biography,
getting aroused by the parts where the shame
and degradation are exactly what he's always wanted,
at a pornographic remove, and his history teacher
knows nothing about the end of Alan Turing's life,
which this boy will wisely leave out of his report.
Chemical castration? *Hot.* Nascent breasts? *Hot.*
Driven to suicide? *Hot. Hot. Hot.* And yes,
in the morning, on the school bus, or in the passenger
seat of his friend-girl's car, he'll think, *That was
seriously fucked up, jerking off to that,* and he won't
even tent his pants by the light of day, knowing
he erased his browser history of all the chastity
blogs, and all the chat rooms where he gets to be
six-foot-two and the captain of the football team
who always just turned eighteen yesterday and
is enslaved to his coach, but that fantasy is getting
tired, and his mind wonders to tomorrow's trig
exam, and soon he'll get back to Alan Turing,
cock-slave to his government. *Hot.* Defeater of Nazis.
Hot. And by day, this you're-not-fooling-anyone
president of the Gay/Straight alliance may be furious
at how this hero was treated, will start a petition
to get the science lab named for Alan Turing,
but at night he wonders, in one recurring fantasy,
if he could ever pass the Turing test, but in the other
direction. If maybe, just maybe, no one could ever tell
he was human.

TYRA HUNTER

You can never know what happened,
not entirely, not fully, but there is
always the trace, the witnesses,
the evidence that you can piece,
the likely version that would explain
her having crawled away from
the paramedics after they stopped
giving her treatment, the witnesses
who maintain that they begged
the paramedics to stop taunting her
and go back to treating her wounds
even as she worked to drag herself
out of the road. There were the nurses
who called her combative, when
she arrived at the hospital,
and the medical records that show
she was treated in accordance
with the protocol for addicts,
despite her clear constitution,
and there is her mother who insists
on her virtue, and it's true that
I am taking sides here, that over
the newspaper accounts through
which her death first reached me,
I was always inclined to side
with Tyra Hunter, to say her name
and to celebrate the life that
she had built in which her boy born
body was treated like the woman
she knew herself to be, until her

car spun out and the EMT
discovered her penis, until
he stopped treating her at the exact
moment, according to witnesses,
he said, "This ain't no bitch,
it's a nigger."

PORNOGRAPHY III

*After James Schuyler's "Things to Do," with lines
from Ben Jonson's* Volpone

Double penetration.
Femdom.
"Dawson's Thousand
Load Weekend."
"The Devil in Miss Jones."
"Jason, please
join me on cam
for the extremely
low rate of three
dollars a minute."
Give head
in any bathroom
when approached.
Respond to all glances
of all men in the street.
And, *now I think on't,*
I will keep thee backwards.
Purchase protection,
condoms,
lube, silicone based,
for heaven's sake,
only silicone based.
Help Debbie do
Dallas. Write
a letter in support
of Linda Lovelace.
Bound Gods
of Bukkake Place.

Remind world
that Shakespeare
was not the only
playwright of
the early modern world.
Text passages from
Edward the Second
to Republican senators.
While naked,
recite Marlowe.
Who can resist
Volpone? Celia
may be the original
anal star.
Being too open,
makes me use you thus.

In the Style of the Master

When he had FINISHED
his project of remaking

there was no gap
between FEAR and GUILT.

The goal was to PLEASE the GOD
who might turn his face

from me;-- and then;--
I turned my face from HIM.

I turned my face from HIM,
and here;-- here;--

among the betrayers
I live out my days

in EXILE.

I Remember

I remember wishing you would stop talking about yourself.

The Worst Children's Book Ever

Seven angels appeared to Kristen after the death of her parents. "We're not angels," they said, but there was no fooling Kristen. "Yes you are," she said. "Please," said the angels, "start a new paragraph for each individual speaker."

New York Schooled Poem for Jen & Ada

Jen & Ada want me to write about being afraid of bears,
probably because Ada is afraid of bears, although maybe
it's Jen who's afraid of bears. Jen's quite tall, and ballsy too.
It's hard for me to imagine Jen being afraid of anything
except irrational and uncontrollable things like aliens & ghosts
& cancer. Unfortunately for our writing group, I am not
afraid of bears, because one really only needs to fear bears
if one plays with bear cubs and the mother bear is nearby.
I do not think that bear cubs are cute, and even if I see them
I am not tempted to play with them, although I think Ada
would be tempted, and come to think of it, she'd be adorable
posed with bear cubs (I'd buy that picture; hell, I'd frame it).
Also, I used to camp a lot in bear country, and I know how to tie
bear bags and dispose of food such that it won't attract
bears. I am scared of many exponents of the animal kingdom,
including spiders, bats, and octopi, but Jen and Ada have been
expressly clear that this poem is only to be about fearing bears.

SCHUYLER-ESQUE

Because today's
to-do list demands
weed whacking, I take
the weed whacker
and whack the weeds
growing between
the bricks of
our patio. Half
the patio done,
Michael says,
"It looks much better"
and "I wish
the patio were level."
A piece of dirt
kicks up at my eye.
Don't worry.
I have eyelids,
and, as it turns out,
excellent reflexes.

WHY WE NEVER WENT BACK TO THE ABSTRACTED FORMS OF GOVERNMENT CAFÉ

For R.S.

Even Communism forgot quite how the fight she was having
with Socialism had led her to think that standing on her chair
and screaming "Pussy Power" would somehow resolve things
in her favor, but there she was, and having already gotten up
on the chair, and having screamed it once, she didn't see anything
else to do, but to keep on screaming it. Socialism was sort of trying
to look away as though being seated at the table wouldn't reveal
that they were there together, and Democracy was so distracted
that she leaned over to Republic and asked when the hell
the god-damned waiter was going to put a stop to this. The way
I'm telling the story, you may not be getting the full effect,
because Communism was actually screaming it over and over
in a rather loud voice, and putting different inflections on the words
as she kept shouting. Matriarchy and Gynarchy were at the bar,
and they stood up to sing "La Marseillaise" as a form of solidarity, an idea
they took from a scene in *Casablanca*, where the prostitute restores
her dignity through patriotism. Oligarchy (the waiter) blamed Monarchy
(the bartender) for making the drinks too strong, and Dictatorship
(the owner) regretted having fired Constitutional Monarchy
(the previous bartender) for making the drinks too weak. "Pussy POWer!
PUSSY power!" screamed Communism, now terrified of what
would happen when she stopped, and certainly, finding yourself
on a chair while screaming "Pussy Power" is embarrassing,
but the moment after you stop is much, much worse.

In the Next Booth

She said, "Remember when you liked me
more than crack?" and he said, "Yeah, that
was when I hadn't met crack yet," and when
she huffed and tried to leave the booth
he grabbed her arm, and pulled her back
and said, "We have to talk about the dog,
remember?" and she said, "I thought
we were talking about the dog?" and he said,
"We have to finish talking about the dog,"
and she said, "So fucking finish talking
about the dog," and he said, "So stop being
a giant cunt and I will," at which point,
in a single sweeping movement of her arm
she knocked every single thing off the table,
and the cups and plates broke against
the floor, and the coffee flew up and stained
my pants, and the silverware clattered, and
we weren't overhearing anymore, we were
paying rapt attention, and he said, "You're paying
for that, you bitch," and she said,
"Pick up the tab, asshole," and not one
single person tried to stop her as she left.

THE BUFFY SESTINA

The First Episode of the New Season, before the Opening Credits.

Buffy is upstairs sharpening her large collection of stakes
when her mother comes upstairs and says, "Would it be bad,
just this once, not to go out staking vampires again tonight?"
After all, she had just defeated an apocalyptic force! Time
for a break? Buffy never has time for a break. Angel gone,
her stakes sharp, she kisses her mom and hops out the window

into the backyard. Buffy is familiar with this small window
at the beginning of every season (school year), when her stakes
are enough to fight her battles, and whatever the big coming
evil will be, it hasn't started to build yet. What big bad
will it be this season? She pulls her coat against the night
and there's Willow! Her best friend! She certainly has time

for Willow! They walk, explicate the summer, say, "Time
to go back to school." Suddenly, a vampire seizes this window
of relaxed defenses, and grabs off-guard Willow. Oh this night-
ly threat! Willow screams and resists. Buffy turns, her stake
at the ready. "Meet my friend, Mr. Pointy!" she says. Bad
bloodsucker, he lets Willow go. He wants to fight. He goes

at Buffy with everything, and Buffy (blue coat, boots) comes
back at him hard. The fight is oddly even. For a long time
(forty seconds, say), he gets in good blows. He hurts her bad,
she looks finished. She isn't getting back up again. A doe
leaps into the cemetery. All are distracted. Willow makes a stake
from a broken bench piece and the vampire tries to run into the night.

But Xander arrives, blocks the exit with his own stake. This night
is going terribly now (for the vampire)! The vampire goes
around to a crypt and tries to run inside, but it takes time
to pry open the gates. Too much time; Xander almost stakes
the vamp, but he stops to quip, and the effort goes bad.
The vampire throws him hard into the boarded-up window

of the crypt. Willow runs over, pulls a board from the window
for a new stake. Buffy's back up. Oh, what a luxury this night
is! Forever to fight just one, lone vampire. Xander's badinage
soundtracks the fight. Willow lunges and misses, coming
close, but too far left. Buffy kicks the vampire in the face, stake
brandished. He goes down, and she's on top of him this time.

Buffy stakes the vampire. He's dust. Whew! Wait. Bad. Crypts
don't have windows. The night is heavy and dark. That took a long time!
What's coming begins to come. Let's un-board that window.

Sita

Do you remember Sita? How when Hanuman came to rescue her
she refused, how she insisted that Rama come openly,
defeat her captor Ravana openly? She had no desire for stealth,
no desire for intrigue, and though Ravana could not touch her
for the curse on his flesh, she remained captive until Rama came.
Do you remember that she was tortured? That Hanuman asked her
for permission to kill the women who had tortured her? Do you
remember how she walked through fire to prove her purity,
even though everyone knew of the curse on Ravana? How the people
said the fire didn't matter because Fire was the brother of her mother,
Earth? How Rama was as weak in the face of his people as he
had been strong in the face of Ravana? Can you imagine the eyes
of Sita when she refused another test? When she looked at Rama,
a man she loved enough to die for, a man who was a god, like she
was a god? Can you imagine her eyes in that moment as she asked
her mother to take her back, to swallow her into the earth? I think
my eyes are like that now, taking my leave from you.

ON LAST LOOKING INTO ASHBERY'S SELF-PORTRAIT

Aren't you dead yet, Mr. Mouth?

Mr. fang-tooth?

Mr. South?

Aren't you dead yet,

Mr. Claw?

Mr. Bosie?

Mr. Shaw?

Are you done breathing

all the air?

Done stealing seats

from every chair?

Enough with vices,

mirrors, trolls.

No more voices,

no more souls.

You're a vampire.

I've got veins.

You're a horse.

Bitch,

I've got reins.

On First Looking into Ashbery's Self-Portrait

That one might speak of the soul so clearly,
without shame or averted eyes, this was cause for awe,
and oh, with eyes so pure we could not help
but covet their vision, did he show us himself conjuring
the past the way a ventriloquist might hold a favorite
dummy on his lap, and it is not that we did not know
the trick, but rather how much we loved the skill
with which the trick was done. Speak of the soul
and we will unlearn fear. Speak of the soul
and we will unlearn speaker, and what you
may speak, oh God, will be the glory of mankind,
and what you may speak, oh God, will teach us
to unlearn ourselves, until there is just voice,
and we forget that only one of us is speaking.

Biographical Note

Photo by Marion Ettlinger

Jason Schneiderman was born in San Antonio, Texas, but was raised around the United States and Western Europe owing to his father's military service. He holds BAs in English and Russian from the University of Maryland, an MFA from NYU, and a PhD from the Graduate Center of CUNY. He is the author of three collections of poems: *Sublimation Point* (Four Way Books, 2004), *Striking Surface* (2010, Ashland Poetry Press, winner of the Richard Snyder Prize), and *Primary Source* (winner of the Benjamin Saltman Award, Red Hen Press, 2016). He is also the editor of the anthology *Queer: A Reader for Writers* (Oxford University Press, 2015). His poetry and essays have appeared in numerous journals and anthologies, including *American Poetry Review, The Best American Poetry, The Bloomsbury Anthology of Contemporary Jewish Poetry, Verse Daily, The Poetry Review,* and *The Penguin Book of the Sonnet*. The American Academy of Poets has featured him as the poet of the day three times, and in 2004, he received the Emily Dickinson Award from the Poetry Society of America. Schneiderman has received Fellowships from the Fine Arts Work Center in Provincetown, Yaddo, and the Bread Loaf Writers Conference. In the fall of 2014, he and Kathryn Maris shared the position of Digital Poet in Residence at the Poetry Campus, based in London. He is an Assistant Professor of English at the Borough of Manhattan Community College and lives in Brooklyn with his husband Michael Broder.

Printed in the USA
CPSIA information can be obtained
at www.ICGtesting.com
JSHW021737300924
70798JS00001B/11